FIND YOUR PEOPLE,
YOUR TOOLS,
AND YOUR VOICE

PALMETTO
PUBLISHING
Charleston, SC
www.PalmettoPublishing.com

Copyright © 2024 by Sima Patel

All rights reserved

No portion of this book may be reproduced, stored in a retrieval system, or transmitted in any form by any means—electronic, mechanical, photocopy, recording, or other—except for brief quotations in printed reviews, without prior permission of the author.

Paperback ISBN: 979-8-8229-4277-6
eBook ISBN: 979-8-8229-4278-3

FIND YOUR PEOPLE, YOUR TOOLS, AND YOUR VOICE

A BLUEPRINT FOR PROFESSIONAL SUCCESS

SIMA PATEL

TABLE OF CONTENTS

Introduction   1

Part I Find Your People   7
   Chapter 1: Get to Know People—Any People   10
   Chapter 2: Walk a Mile in Someone Else's Shoes   14
   Chapter 3: Communication and Trust   20

Part II Find Your Tools   33
   Chapter 4: Core Values   35
   Chapter 5: Get Stuff Done   42
   Chapter 6: Dress for Success   51

Part III Find Your Voice   57
   Chapter 7: Give Yourself a Break   60
   Chapter 8: Remind Yourself Every Day Why You are so Amazing   65
   Chapter 9: Have the Courage to Fight for Yourself   68

Conclusion   79
Acknowledgments   84
My Favorite Leadership Books   93

INTRODUCTION

I'm an Indian woman, the one who had very traditional Indian parents who moved to the US a long time ago. In my case, it was in 1970 when my parents moved to America. I was a bridge kid, that's my first identity. But, add to that, I'm a mom of two of my own kids, a wife for twenty-one-plus years, a daughter, a sister, an aunt, a friend, a team member, a leader, and a mentor. Also, I have a full-time job as a Chief of Staff for a publicly traded company. That's a lot of hats. And for all these hats, I take my responsibilities very seriously. Sometimes I look at my kids—who are now in high school and middle school—and wonder how in the world I ever got through while working full-time and having a very demanding career. It's a very delicate dance to balance what I call "home hats" while pushing yourself to grow and pursue your "work hats" for your career and dreams. Historically, my culture has been much more welcoming to men in the workplace, resulting in a male-dominated workforce. So, growing up (despite my progressive parents who were always so supportive), the messages around me were more about being a good Indian girl, getting married, having babies, and being a part of the Indian community.

As an American-born, very traditionally raised girl who grew up in the '80s and '90s, life was so different for me than it is for my daughter, who is now fifteen. I always felt like I had to claw my way up, dodging the roadblocks of not really being "American" and not being male, so two strikes against me. My daughter, however, celebrates her culture and has flawlessly found a way to appreciate being both American and Indian. Probably because the world she lives in accepts other cultures, and in her eyes, she's no different from anyone else. Those two strikes against me are instead two check marks of diversity for her.

Feeling like you have something to prove can sometimes be the best motivator. Maybe that's why I work extra hard and why my accomplishments feel even more deserved. It's been really important for me to grow my career because, while I live to do things for other people, my career is my own, and I do it for myself. It brings me so much gratitude and personal satisfaction. I want my daughter to know she really can do anything she sets her mind to and my son to see how powerful women are. I want them to see that you can have both a successful career and be everything to everyone that's most important in your life at the same time.

And that brings me to why I wrote this book. Thinking back on my career, I've had over twenty years of experience in sales and operations, spanning multiple industries, including: media, wine/beverage, medical equipment, commercial construction, professional services, software as a service (SaaS), a bakery, hotels/motels, and a franchise restaurant. All these moments taught me pieces of information that I have carried, used, and cherished. Even the worst—and I mean absolute worst—of times taught the greatest lessons that I value so much now (not so much while they were happening, though).

I wanted to leave behind something that will help people get to where they want to be in their own careers. I've learned to navigate work dynamics, handle complex situations, and have difficult conversations. Success is such a subjective word, and it means different things to different people, so I don't like to throw it around casually. But I've been successful by my own standards, and I believe my advice can relate to a lot of people. I want to offer words of wisdom and life experiences that maybe my kids and future grandkids can learn from. I know I learned a lot from my grandfather Bhulabhai Patel; he was an inspiration to me and to many women. He left a legacy that is still impacting hundreds of girls in the rural villages of Gujarat, India.

Bhulabhai's Story:

My grandparents' marriage was already arranged when my grandfather was two and while my great-grandmother was pregnant with my grandmother. When my grandmother was born, tragically, her mother died during childbirth. Her father died when she was just seven. As an only child with no other family, her young groom's family took her in, sealed the marriage to my grandfather, and raised her. They grew up together and supported each other.

My grandfather, Bhulabhai Patel, was smart and ambitious, but his parents were poor and couldn't afford an education past middle school. In those days in India, you had to pay for high school in addition to college. My grandmother decided to sell what gold and jewelry she had inherited from her parents to put my grandfather through school. He became a very successful senator. He led rallies to fight for women's rights and always gave back to those less fortunate than he was. Using his influence, he felt like he could do so much more than what he was already doing. So, after discussing it with his wife and three kids (my aunt, uncle, and my mom), he made the decision to downsize their lifestyle so he could make a bigger impact.

Education for girls in the '50s in India was very rare, but he believed in equality. He used to always say that his daughters should get the same education as his son. At that time, it was taboo for girls to leave a village for school, but that was what they had to do to receive a high school or college education. My grandfather had the brilliant idea to build a school in the village, free of fees, to allow these bright young girls to get the education they deserved. The school was wildly successful, and through generous donations, he and his partners were able to build four more schools. In 2018, statues of him and his partners were placed at their first school to honor the great work they did. My kids, my husband, and I visited the first school he built (where my mom was a teacher). To meet a new generation of girls who would receive a full education there, over sixty years later was profoundly gratifying. Our family has a strong line of powerhouse women, and I got to see where it all comes from.

My grandfather died at the age of eighty when I was sixteen, and three weeks later, my grandmother died of a broken heart. He has been gone for nearly thirty years, but his legacy and great impact live on.

While my journey and impact can't compare to what he's done, I hope this book will help someone in some small way. People have asked me what things I've done and how I've progressed in my career. I find that there are three things I do in every job I've ever had, in my personal life, and in every relationship I carry. This monograph is made up of three parts, representing each of those three areas:

Part 1: Find Your People. Grow your network and find the people who will help you succeed.

Part 2: Find Your Tools. These are the tools you need to be successful in getting things done.

Part 3: Find Your Voice. Kill your head trash, otherwise known as imposter syndrome, and get out of your way.

I'm going to end this note by telling you what my dad always tells me: "Sima, treat advice like a buffet. Take everything on your plate and sample it. Eat what you like, and throw the rest away." So while this book is full of advice, use what makes sense to you and disregard the rest.

PART I

FIND YOUR PEOPLE

Think back to your first day of work. It can be your first job or your last job—the story is pretty much the same. You wake up with exhilaration! You have your supplies ready, your first-day-of-work outfit picked out, coffee in hand, and you are going to conquer the world!

You get to work and look around, and slowly that feeling drains just a little bit. You realize you don't know anyone, and people don't know you. They don't know how amazing you are and how hard you're going to work. You have to start at square one and prove yourself. It feels a bit like an uphill battle. Whether you work at a big company or a small one, that feeling is kind of the same.

I remember feeling like that every time I started a new job, no matter what position I was in or where I was on the org chart. I always wanted to be heard, to contribute, and to add value. It never seemed to happen fast enough; I wanted to get there yesterday. I would look around and think, how do I, a guppy in this massive ocean, find my way? It took me years to realize some things I did organically were actually strategic all along. Ever since I can remember, I've been a naturally curious person who loves to learn, and every time I started a new job, I unknowingly began by finding my people.

When I say "find your people", I mean, build meaningful relationships and trust with the right people who will help you succeed at work. These are people who you want to invest in a relationship with. Get to know them, respect their work and their processes, and collaborate on how you can work together. Finding your people takes time; it doesn't happen overnight. It takes patience, mutual respect, understanding, and teamwork. The longer you are at your organization, the stronger and larger your community becomes. It must be done with intention and planning, not by chance.

If you're in a people-leadership position, your people consist of not only peers but your team as well. Their success is ultimately your success.

Here are three key tips to help you build relationships and **find your people**:

1. Get to know people and how their team operates.
2. Have empathy for others; don't be quick to assume.
3. Build trust through honesty and transparency whenever possible.

CHAPTER 1

GET TO KNOW PEOPLE— ANY PEOPLE

You have to be intentional when it comes to building relationships at work. Sure, there are those you'll instantly connect with who become your friends, and that's great! But you also need alliances and friends in other spaces throughout the organization, because you never know when your paths will cross.

The number of times my path crossed with someone in a seemingly random encounter who ended up being an important part of my journey is indescribably delightful. I once ended up working for someone I coincidentally ran into in an elevator (so glad I introduced myself and made a good impression). Take every opportunity to introduce yourself; believe me, they will remember you.

At the end of the day, the whole organization is one entity; each of the different departments is necessary for an organization to be successful. As cliché as it sounds, think of an orchestra. All the instruments play their different parts, but from the outside, it sounds like a unified piece of music.

It's overwhelming in the beginning. You may not know a lot of people, which makes it hard to know where to start. It could be that you're new or that you've worked in one department for so long that you only interact with those people. Figure out how your department works with others, because they're not all built the same. Why do this? Because understanding how the organization works, and how your department interacts with others, instantly changes your perspective on your own work. Knowing the high-level basics of how the organization operates will put you miles ahead of other people because you'll be able to add more insight when helping make decisions.

How do you start? It's always good to begin with your manager. Let them know you want to learn and grow in your role, meet other people, and get to know the organization and how it works. Ask for names or introductions to help you get started. If they aren't helpful, take the initiative yourself. Pull up your organizational chart and study it. Who reports to who? How are the dots connected? Once you figure out where you want to put your time and energy, start reaching out. Typically, you never start with people at the top; they are way too busy, and you'll get lost in the shuffle. Keep going down the organizational chart and look for titles like "team lead" or "manager." If there is a chief of staff or business operations manager, reach out to them with your request. They will know who you should contact. (There is an example of this in the exercise at the end of Part I).

Setting up and having these conversations accomplishes three things:
- You meet someone new you wouldn't normally talk with (this expands your network).
- You learn how a process works and how your team fits in with theirs (this gains knowledge and respect).

- You build relational equity (they're more willing and positioned to help you).

The next time you need help, you will know how that team operates so you'll be able to plan, prepare, and tailor your request accordingly. This will make you more efficient with your time, and your network will be more willing to help expedite your requests on urgent matters (just don't abuse it).

Recognizing and understanding how to build strategic relationships that relate to your work is crucial, and don't forget other areas of the organization that are equally important and often overlooked. A very important and most of the time unseen team is Information Technology (IT)! Be *especially* kind and get to know them. They are in a grind! They spend all day putting out fires and tending to urgent requests. Most of the time, they are the least appreciated and most overlooked team. A smile and a nice gesture goes a long way.

I was walking through the office one day and walked past the IT area. I felt so bad for them—they looked exhausted. I could see the multiple faulty computers being tested, hear the new notifications pouring in for tech support, and it was apparent that they were understaffed. All I did was smile, say hi, genuinely ask how their day was going, and thank them for all the great work they were doing. That was all. They told me people don't usually say thank you, much less stop and say hi. They really appreciated being appreciated! It was just a gesture, but it made them feel good. I was shocked that people don't just do that; this is an important (mission critical) team! Where would we be without IT? Since then, anytime I need something from IT, they always help me. Let me be clear, I didn't stop and appreciate them so they would help me. I did it because they really do a lot and they should be told how important they are. So please, tell your IT team how amazing they are!

In addition to getting to know people, it's a really good idea to get to know the products and services your company sells (assuming you're not in a product/sales role and already know your stuff). When was the last time you actually used your company's product to experience its value, quality, and utility? I say that because the more you know about your company and what it does, the more you can make conscious decisions on how you run your business, and how it can add value to the organization as a whole. Frankly, it doesn't matter what department you're in. You will be so much more confident speaking about your work and what your company does for other people, and this will build your credibility.

CHAPTER 2

WALK A MILE IN SOMEONE ELSE'S SHOES

Earlier I mentioned the importance of understanding how your company works. From a very broad perspective, there are two key functions of any organization: revenue generation and revenue protection. Revenue generation is pretty much all sales-related activities, and revenue protection encompasses everything else. *Every company is a sales company.* I'm going to stop for a minute to let that sink in: *Every company is a sales company.*

If you're in a sales role reading this, you're probably really excited to see that, and maybe you feel a bit validated. If you're not, you may not appreciate what I just said. Whether you like it or not, it's true. No company can exist if they don't have sales, so generally speaking, all resources will usually be determined by how sales are performing. You'll notice that if sales are down, support functions and resources get cut while the company hires for sales positions. (On a side note, that's not always the best move. Sure, you'll get the sales, but with support resources cut, in the long run, you'll lose customers and renewals.)

That's not to say that the product, engineering, and other departments are not important. If you don't have a product, what are you selling? Product and engineering teams have to work closely with the sales department so they get feedback directly from customers and can make improvements. Legal and compliance departments exist to keep the company from paying fines and facing adverse legal action. The human resources department is important to take care of employees and continue hiring the right talent. The point is that all of these departments really have to work together to support each other.

But there has always been this unspoken angst between salespeople and operations people. They don't always like each other because they don't *understand* one another. As a person who started out in sales, I know sellers. I *get* sellers. That's what makes me an effective operations leader. It's hard out there, and it's *not* glamorous. In fact, it's the opposite. It's a grind and extremely stressful. You have to work really hard to make your quota every month. say you hit your number one month - *Boom*! On the first day of the following month, you have to start over again. If you don't make your numbers, it could impact your personal income, which then affects your ability to pay the rent or mortgage, take a vacation, or pay for extracurricular activities for your kids.

On the other hand, it's hard being in a supporting role. You get slammed with "urgent" requests all day long, especially at the end of the month. The business wants you to make mountains move with your imaginary magic wand—surprise – it's not going to happen. And then you have to say the dreaded "no". It's not what the customer, seller,

seller's manager, seller's manager's manager, CEO, etc. want to hear. Company revenue pays for everything, but the operations team has to deliver what was sold. Sometimes there is a disconnect between what we say we're going to do and what we can actually do.

And that's how the war starts. Both sides of the coin think they have the harder job, and they each do. It builds a rift, it's distracting, and actual work isn't happening because of emotions and feelings. But sales and operations are a symbiotic relationship. Neither can exist without the other. So, what if they could appreciate each other and work together? Who benefits (besides both parties and the organization as a whole)? The actual customer! This is easy to say and hard to do.

> *I worked for an organization where I ran the operations for a district and had little to do with the sales. I could see that there was definitely a rift between both parties. For the sake of privacy, let's call our seller Bill and our customer service representative (CSR) John.*
>
> *Bill rolled into the office in the afternoon looking sharp with his pressed shirt and sunglasses on. He slammed down paperwork (not noticing that John's eyebrows were scrunched up intensely and he was fiercely typing on his computer, while the phone was ringing). Bill just started talking.*
>
> *"So, I need you to process this paperwork for my order. And can you give me an update on…"*
>
> *Bill might as well have said "blah blah blah," because John didn't give a rip. It was clear that John wasn't listening. So, Bill grumbled something under his breath and walked away in a huff. I asked Bill what happened and why he was so angry.*

"He never listens to me! I have orders that need to get processed. I spent all day waiting in a doctor's office for the doctor to sign this order for oxygen tanks, and John doesn't care. I don't have the luxury of sitting around in the warm office. I have to go out and fight traffic, driving from one office to another, hoping I can get orders so I make my quota. John doesn't have to stress out, he gets paid regardless."

I looked at him and said, "Whoa! Hold on there, do you know how hard it is to do what he's doing? He's got orders to process, he's working the phones, helping walk-ins, managing other ad hoc work, and he gets interrupted all day long, much like you just did." Bill gave me a look, didn't say anything and just walked off.

Later that day, I went to John, and I asked him if he'd processed Bill's order.

"Nope, I'll get to it when I get to it," he said dryly.

John began to complain about how Bill doesn't appreciate the work he does. "Bill comes in all high and mighty because he's in sales. He gets to get out of the office, take people out to lunch, and schmoozes people all day. I'm stuck here in this office trying to manage phones with angry customers, people walking in, and processing orders. I don't have the luxury of just hanging out all day like he does."

Interesting. They both thought the other person had it easier. I decided to "run a leadership experiment". Since Bill didn't report to me, I had to get permission from his boss, the district sales manager. He agreed to my little experiment.. So, I pulled both Bill and John aside and replayed what had happened that day from each of their perspectives. I told them that they both thought the other had a more luxurious day and, in fact, they were both right and *wrong at the same time. Both jobs are hard work, and instead of working together and giving in a bit more, they were making it so much harder for themselves. I let them know they were each going to spend a full day with one another. The next day, John was to accompany Bill in the field for the whole day trying to get orders signed. I would play CSR for the day. The day after that, Bill would sit with John the whole day and juggle phones, walk-ins, and orders.*

Forty-eight hours later, after both Bill and John had spent the day with each other, their interactions were like night and day. Bill came in from the field and waited until John was off the phone, rather than interrupting. He said things like "please" and "thank you," instead of demanding assistance. He also brought John a coffee as an appreciation. Similarly, John began to prioritize Bill's orders and was equally friendly with him. I asked them what they learned from the experiment, and both replied that they had no idea how hard the other's job was. John said he would go crazy if he had that kind of pressure and had to wait around in a doctor's office at their mercy. Bill said he couldn't possibly be as organized and manage all the things that had to be done each day in the office. I'm not saying there was never friction again, but it was met with much more kindness, mutual respect, and grace than ever before. One thing I have learned about leadership: run experiments to build strong teams! You may come end up right, you may end up wrong- but either way, you'll have learned something.

Knowing how other teams operate while understanding and respecting their SLA's (service level agreements, a fancy way to say turnaround time) allows you to be in their good grace. Being empathetic to what they endure makes others instantly go from being defensive to wanting to help you.

So, the moral of that story is that until you experience what other people are going through, you likely can't appreciate them. Once you do understand, you begin to give them more grace and practice patience. When you start seeing things from a different lens, it does wonders for the work you produce. It clears up misunderstandings, eliminates unnecessary friction, and promotes a much more productive work environment.

Think about someone at work who has been really frustrating you. Stop for a minute and ask them questions about what their world is like. Learning the things they have to go through and endure will help you navigate how you interact with them. Remember that you catch more bees with honey than vinegar, and always keep your goal in mind. What is the problem you (or they!) are trying to solve?

Sometimes it means that you take a step back and realize that working with someone is more important than being right. That means, as much as you want to raise your voice, or really, really prove your point- you have to ask yourself, is it worth it? Because nine times out of ten, it probably isn't. Remember how it feels to receive feedback? You want someone to be nice, explain it calmly, and sympathize with you. Well, that's how EVERYONE wants to be treated.

CHAPTER 3

COMMUNICATION AND TRUST

So much time is wasted on assumptions and unstated or unconfirmed expectations. Assumptions generally happen with a lack of information or communication and can turn into the most horrific misunderstandings. I'm getting an image of the '70s TV show *Three's Company* as I'm writing this. Basically, each episode is a giant misunderstanding where someone says something and the other person overhears it and interprets it a different way with zero context. This causes massive confusion and begins a domino effect until, finally, it all comes to a head, and they actually talk and laugh about it in the end. Because it's on TV, it's quite comical. But this is real life, so assumptions can lead to a lot of damage and most of the time won't be solved in thirty minutes like they are on the show.

People Leaders
If you're a people leader, work *with* your team. It's your job to communicate and be as transparent as you can. Look, I understand you can't tell them *everything*. But you can find a filter and give them the story and the

why behind it. I cannot reiterate enough *how important* this is. It seems so simple, and yet when faced with those situations, we tend to want to withhold information.

The reason I'm calling this out specifically is because trust is so delicate. You could do everything right and build a fantastic culture, but one wrong move when it counts will dramatically and negatively affect your team. Communication and information are the key components to building and *keeping* trust. Trust is also cumulative, you build it daily and it compounds through time as they get to know your character as their leader. You will make mistakes and the cumulative trust will get you through these mistakes as you apologize and move forward. Build your trust bank, save up for the really big decisions that will drain trust as you lead your organization through them (e.g. downsizing in adversity).

Here's an example: It's nearing the end of the quarter, and you're nowhere near reaching the goal that was set for your team. The clock is ticking, but the team just isn't producing what's required. You sit down by yourself and think of the different ways you can solve this. Do you implement a cash incentive to get people motivated? Do you tell the team they just need to get this done? This is their job though, right? No one should question it or have to know why. You choose not to consult with them for the best solution. Instead, you pull your team together after you've unilaterally decided on one or more of the options above - and you tell them what needs to happen.

The outcome? Maybe you're lucky and they pull through at the end, so you think it's a win. But, ultimately, operating in that way causes you to lose your credibility. Why, you wonder? Well, because you lost out on the opportunity to bring your team in and allow them to help solve the problem *together*. Your people want to be empowered. They want to be a part of the process; they are experts, after all, in what they're doing, and asking them for their input will go a long way! They will take real ownership of their work and care more about the results if they are part of the decision-making process. If your team comes up with the idea, they are more likely to get their peers to buy in and implement it. It also boosts their confidence and allows them to learn how to make decisions so they don't come to you for every little thing. Asking can be part of your leadership competitive edge.

> *I worked for an organization going through an accreditation process, and at some point, the accreditation company was going to show up at our office and quiz the team on approved practices to make sure we met their standards. There was some theory work. but mostly it was a lot of memorization, and we had maybe five weeks to fully prepare. I held a meeting with the whole team to brainstorm how we were going to tackle this. They had so many great and creative ideas—from quizzing each other to holding a game show with dollar scratchers as prizes for answers that were correct.*
>
> *It brought everyone together and gave them a chance to build each other up. I would never have thought of that! When the issue originally came to me, I assumed the team would probably be frustrated and not want to do it. But they really surprised me, and instead of it being a chore, it was fun! Not only that, but we also excelled in our interviews and impressed the auditor so much that the chief compliance officer reached out to personally thank our center for our efforts.*

The concept of sharing and communicating stands true, especially in times of turmoil. Many companies go through delicate times, and the economy plays a huge role in that. No matter how great your product or organization is, it's bound to be affected in some way during an unfortunate economic landscape. It's in those times that communication and trust play a massive role in how you will prevail in the end. Most of the time, the situation is beyond your control, and it's hard to share bad news, so your instinct is sometimes to bury it or glaze it over instead of just being honest. But it's your job to be as transparent as you can be.

In the absence of information, people will *always* make things up. Their conclusions generally start with whatever pieces of information they do have, filtered through their own lenses. And then they all share with each other. Yes, your team is 100 percent talking about what they think is going on, and they all have a different version of what it could be. Now, I will say, there are bits of information you probably can't and shouldn't share, and that's okay. Tell your team the information you can share without getting into the details; give them enough context so they're not completely in the dark or blindsided. That way they can walk away having some sort of clarity instead of a distorted reality.

It's so easy to make things up in our heads. Think back to the last few disagreements you might have had with someone. How many of those were the direct result of a lack of communication and information? It's something so trivial that could grow into something massive.

The typical equation goes like this:

lack of information → making assumptions → start "seeing" the evidence for it = distorted version of reality, wasted time, negative emotions, and negative actions.

By far the most important thing to do is to acknowledge your team members' feelings. Most of the time, people just want to be heard. It's okay to ask them if they want you to take action on their feedback or if they just want you to listen. They're not dumb, they know it might not have been your decision to make. This is how you build trust. It's a lesson I've learned the hard way in my career. Once you lose trust, it's almost impossible (very, very hard and costly) to get it back.

> *I worked for a small company where I was the chief operations officer. We were going through financially tough times. As a leader, I was trying to put on a brave face. I didn't always share things with my people, and I pretended like everything was okay because I didn't want to worry them. The stress definitely brought out the worst in me. I made poor decisions, and I didn't communicate properly. I thought if I shared too much, they would all leave and I would be in a worse position. So, I gave my team incomplete information and glossed over the gravity of the situation.*
>
> *They knew things were not okay, and they most definitely discussed it among themselves. It created a great distance between me and them, and over time, the separation just got bigger and bigger because they never knew if they were getting all the information they needed. My decision to protect them by not sharing led to them not trusting me. I tried many times to overcome that, but it was never quite the same. In hindsight, I should have brought them in and told them the gist of what was actually going on. They would likely have helped me come up with solutions. At the very least, it would have brought us together.*

When you have to deliver news that's not so awesome, do it truthfully and with kindness. Most people want to avoid difficult conversations like the plague. I imagine there are very few people who wake up and say, "Yes! I get to crush someone's world today!" But the very best people leaders are able to put their emotions aside and have direct, kind conversations.

When I worked for a media company, I was a co-manager with someone who happened to become one of my best friends. For privacy purposes, let's call her Allie. To this day, I've never been more in sync and aligned with someone in a working relationship than I was with Allie. Co-managing our team could have been a recipe for disaster, but it wasn't. It was the epitome of what a real collaborative work friendship could look like. Allie was an absolute genius in digital strategy. I was not—like, not even close. I was, however, a very experienced operations leader. After we had gone through several directors of operations (they just couldn't seem to cut it), our leadership realized one of us should be the operations director.

We both interviewed for it, and we knew one of us would get this job. Because of my experience, I wrongly assumed I should get the position. I prepared for the interview, I thought I aced it, and then I didn't get the job. Allie did. I was devastated and confused. I took a moment to pull myself together, and then my boss did me a solid. He told me why I didn't get the job. While he agreed I was more experienced in leading teams and operations, the organization was really looking for the person in this role to lead the digital strategy.

I instantly felt better and wholeheartedly agreed that Allie was the right person for the role and there was no one better suited than her. If my boss hadn't told me the truth and given me the context I needed, it could have not only created a rift in my friendship with Allie (obviously for my own selfish reasons—nothing she did wrong), it would have greatly diminished my confidence. In case you're wondering, Allie and I are still great friends! She is someone I have learned so much from and truly admire as a leader.

It doesn't always work out that way, though. You don't always get the right context, and you can see what major effect it would have had on me had he not shared those few sentences of context. Oftentimes, we try to spare feelings by not saying something, but in the end, it's more selfish not to tell the truth. You have no idea what a positive impact you might have on someone (even though it was difficult to deliver at the time). In the case of my example above, with Allie and the operations role, I was able to move forward with my self-respect and dignity, because I knew not getting that job wasn't about something I lacked personally. I just didn't have the right experience for what the organization needed at the time. Being vulnerable and telling the "transparent truth" requires personal trust and courage. It's what great leaders do.

Individual Contributors

If you're an individual contributor (IC), try not to assume anything if you aren't getting information. I know how hard this is! Instead, ask first, always. Generally speaking, if you look your leader in the eye and ask them directly what the context is, you may not get the full picture, but there is a good chance they will give you some information to work from.

Sometimes, you have to be your own advocate. Suggest to your manager that you have a group brainstorm to find a solution. This shows initiative and will solidify you as a trusted leader in the group, not only with your peers but with your manager, as well. Information and context are incredibly important, not only for producing quality work but also for relationships.

Getting to know people, having true empathy for others, and building trust through communication and teamwork will undoubtedly make you a leader, whether you manage a team or not. People will look to you as a powerful and well-connected force, which is a better position to be in than just having the title and authority. Remember that cream always rises to the top. You will become an asset to your manager, your team, and the organization as a whole. You might not have started out in a big role, but you get to make that role as big as you want. And when there is an opportunity for a promotion, the odds are in your favor.

The work you do in getting to know people, understanding your organization, and building trust all lead to you naturally having people you can count on to help you when you need it. It's a symbiotic relationship. While it's not something that will happen overnight, it's worth the wait and hard work you put into building your network. I've always believed that you don't have to be good at everything (no one is). Align yourself with people who are good at the things you're not so you can be a powerful team together.

You never have to (and won't) know everything or how everything works. You just need to know who to go to for what and trust that they have your back (just as you'll have theirs!). These are your people.

FIND YOUR PEOPLE EXERCISE

1. **Choose your network..**
   - Start with your manager and ask whom you should talk to.
   - If you're on your own, or in conjunction with your manager's recommendations, pull up your organizational chart. Write down what areas of work or departments touch your area of work and how they interact with your department.
   - Make a list of key people in those departments.
     - ▶ Your mind might go right to the top of the food chain in that department, but that's not the best place to start. Start in the middle to find someone who is accessible and might have the bandwidth to talk with you.

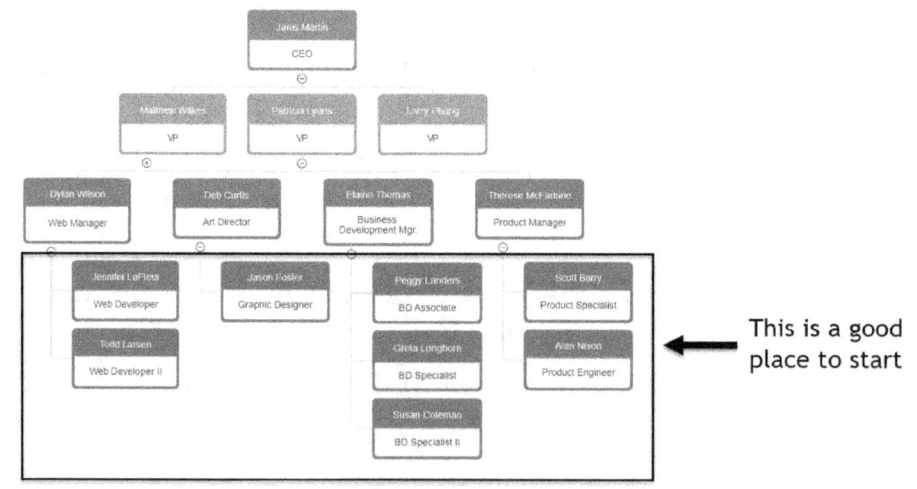

Example organizational chart

2. **Make contact.**
   - Send an email or direct message to the person you want to talk with to let them know who you are, what you're trying to accomplish, and request a meeting.
     - *For example: "Hi! My name is _____ and I work in _____ department. I'm new here (or I'm new to ____ team), and I think we will be working together on various projects along the way. I would love to take a few minutes to get to know you and learn how best to work together.*
   - If they agree, set up a thirty-minute meeting. Most of the time you can check their calendar to see when they are busy or free.

3. **Prepare for the meeting.**
   - Here are sample questions to ask your new contact at your upcoming meeting.
     - *Tell me about yourself, how long you've been here, and what your journey has been like.*
     - *How will we be working together?*
     - *Are there certain processes your team follows I should be aware of?*
     - *What are things I can do to help you?*
     - *If I ever have questions, can I reach out and ask you?*
     - *Is there anyone else on your team I should get to know?*
     - *Is there anything else I should know?*
   - Add any other questions that feel relevant to you!

4. **Attend the meeting.**
   - Make sure to take notes during your meeting.
   - Set a time to have a follow up conversation if it feels relevant. You might suggest a bi-monthly or quarterly meeting if it's appropriate.

5. **Follow up after the meeting.**
   - Via direct message, if possible, thank them for the meeting (email might feel too formal). *You could say, "Thanks so much for meeting with me! I really liked learning about____ "* or whatever is relevant from your meeting. Keep it short and snappy. Alternatively, hand write a short thank you note...this will create differentiation and be memorable in your relationship, and leadership!
   - Go back to your notes to summarize and clean up what you captured. The notes should make sense if you come back to them months later.

6. **Stay in Touch.**
   - Place on your calendar, a recurring reminder to reach out to them with a brief email, text, note or meeting. Finding your people is about building relationships and creating value. Make these deposits into the relationship bank and the rest will flow naturally.

Points to remember:
- Be mindful of when you are asking for the meeting. It's best to avoid setting a meeting for the end of the month, quarter, or year. I always say shoot for the second week of the month, if possible. Confirm what time zone they are in as well. There's nothing worse than accidentally setting up a 5:00 a.m. meeting.
- Be genuine and ask questions in your own words. It shouldn't sound unnatural.
- Use a digital tool to capture your notes like Evernote or OneNote. (You'll learn more about the best tools to use in Part II: Use Your Weapons). Be careful to be present when using technology! While you take notes digitally, you want the other person to know you're listening and are 100% committed.
- If you agreed on any action items during the meeting, be sure to follow through on them. This is very important because it leaves the right impression and exemplifies your value and accountability. (You'll learn ways to organize and follow through in Part II: Find Your Tools).

PART II
FIND YOUR TOOLS

As you build your network, think about where you can add value to your people. This is all a part of building credibility with others, which is your own personal brand in the organization. Think about the people you like to work with and why you like to work with them. Do they always get stuff done? Are they go-getters? Are they helpful to others? What do you want people to say about you? Using the right "tools" to help define yourself and the value you bring to the table is crucial.

I use "tools" loosely here because it means so many things. Tools are the technical platforms you use that make your life easier, your core values, and how you represent yourself. Basically, tools are everything you do, who you are, and how you handle situations. They're also how you get things done. All of these tools build your brand and buy you equity with others.

Think about it this way, pretend you are building a team and you need the right people to get a job done. Automatically you're probably picturing specific people who you've worked with in the past - who come to the table with solutions, or people who always get stuff done. Those are the people you want on your team. The faces of those people came to your mind because they've built the reputation of being people that can be counted on. Building that reputation takes time, patience, and lots of effort. Your tools will help you get there!

Your tools can be divided into three areas:

1. Define your core values and embrace the important role they play in your life.
2. Assemble the tools and technology you need to help track and stay on top of your work.
3. Build confidence in how you present yourself.

CHAPTER 4

CORE VALUES

Everything starts with your core values because they guide your decision-making. Core values are intrinsically who you are. Everyone has core values, they just may not have defined them. I get that it sounds like such a buzzword. But it's a fancy way of saying your non-negotiables—who you are and how you live your life. It's almost like a voice inside you that tells you what's important to you. Core values are not the same for everyone, and they may change as you embrace what's important to you.

Here are some personal core values that guide my life:

- **Live with integrity.**
  Do the right thing, even when no one is watching. Always tell the truth. Don't lie. Don't steal. Don't cheat. These are probably things you learned at home growing up or in kindergarten—the very basics of being a good person. I'm a really bad liar, and I feel awful if I've hurt someone or done something I know is wrong. It just sits and festers, so instead I try to do the right thing even when I don't want to.

- **Help others and be kind.**
  The universe will take care of you; your job is to help others. I've been very blessed in my life, so I believe I have to help people. If I do one small thing for someone, it could make a big difference in their life. Because my goal is to positively impact people, I like to take every opportunity to do that. Call it karma, but the more kindness I've put out in the world, somehow, it's found its way back to me when I needed it.

- **Figure it out.**
  No matter what the situation is, most of the time you don't get a roadmap. Learn to read the room and create your own map with directions to find a way.

  This became a core value by accident. Being thrown into eight different industries meant that I had to learn quickly. I pretty much never know what I'm doing, but I've gotten really good at figuring it out. If you can look at the big picture and focus on understanding the situation and the goal, you can probably figure out what you need to do, or turn to your people when you need help. It takes time and practice.

- **Take accountability.**
  Take 100 percent ownership, whether it's good or bad, especially when it may hurt. Learn to apologize sincerely and do what you say you're going to do.

I remember one very big mistake I made at work once. I was newish, and my job was to project manage working with our sellers to move all our customers off our old platform and transition them to our new platform. I thought I had it all under control, and we were right on schedule. Until I got an email from one of our directors asking me what the plan was for all of our auto renewals. I stopped in my tracks. I knew about the auto renewals, I just forgot about them. This was so uncharacteristic of me, I am always on top of my business. I have no idea how I missed this.

I panicked, immediately called my boss, and told him what was going on. He told me he would have my back and help me (see how he was living his core values?). We would need to propose a plan and meet with our chief operating officer (COO). At that point, I was literally shaking, because our COO didn't know me that well, and my first meeting with him was going to include sitting in front of him and telling him what a dummy I was. But I put my big girl pants on, and I did it.

All of us were in a Zoom room, and I started the meeting by telling him, in front of everyone, that I was really sorry, and that I had messed up. He responded by smiling at me and telling me it was okay. Then he rattled off some solutions like it was no big deal. Let me tell you, it was actually a big deal! But because I took accountability and sincerely apologized from the start, he appreciated it and probably respected me more. Instantly, I felt better, and a huge weight lifted off me. I executed the rest of the project, and it all ended well. Taking accountability builds respect, loyalty and admiration.

- **Be brave and get comfortable with being uncomfortable.**
  This is when the best learning happens; you will never grow in your comfort zone. This one is tough because it requires being vulnerable. If you want to grow, you have to get uncomfortable. Think back to all the times you learned something or did something that was difficult. In the moment, you may not have enjoyed it, but afterward, were you proud of yourself? That right there is the feeling that you want to remember when you're in challenging situations. Truthfully, writing this monograph absolutely terrifies me and puts me in an uncomfortable situation. Writing about things I have gone through (including my mistakes) for other people to read is scary. It makes me feel so naked. But I don't regret it.

- **Persistence pays off.**
  Work hard and don't give up. Do the things you don't want to do but know you need to. Life is not easy, and nothing great comes from easy. The most amazing things in life are born from hard work, and the reward is equally satisfying because of it.

In 2021, I really wanted to work at my current company. I spent a few years following its success, and I watched the company grow and acquire other organizations then go public. I also appreciated that the company core values matched my personal core values. After mailing (yes, I said mailing, not emailing) the CEO my resume, he actually responded and had his chief HR officer meet with me. It was a great informational interview, and about a month later I saw a post for a program manager position that fit exactly what I was looking for. I reached back out to her, and she put me in touch with the hiring manager.

I went through four interviews in five days, and I loved every minute. Some of the interviews were slated for thirty minutes, but we talked for an hour instead. I was so sure I got the job. And then I didn't. I didn't get the job. I can't even describe how devastated I was. They were honest with me, though, which I truly appreciated. I learned that I would be a great culture fit but I didn't have the technical skills they were looking for to be a program manager. I sulked for a few days and really thought about what I wanted to do. I decided I wasn't going to take no for an answer, and I was going to go out and get those technical skills by getting my Project Management Professional (PMP) certification.

I signed up for the preparatory course and felt really excited to learn. Then the class started, and I didn't understand anything the instructor was talking about—like, at all. He might as well have been talking in a foreign language. I felt so discouraged and really wanted to give up, but I trudged along and did the reading and exercises. After the class was done, I reread the textbook, took more practice quizzes, and studied for three more months. I took the four-hour exam on a Sunday with knots in my stomach. As I was taking the exam, I felt like it was too easy (it wasn't easy, I was just extremely prepared for it). I killed that exam. I scored in the ninetieth percentile in each of the three areas: people, process, and business. I couldn't believe it!

I had so much adrenaline in me that I woke up at 5:00 a.m. the next morning and emailed the four people who I had interviewed with. I basically told them what I had done and that I still

> *wanted to work there. I told them if they hired me, they would be getting someone who wouldn't give up and who would find a way. A few hours later, I got a response and a request to meet again later that day. So, I met with a couple more people.* **I got the job**. *If that wasn't satisfying enough, at least I know when I tell my kids never to give up on what they want- they have seen what that really means.*

One last point on core values is that you have to work for a company that has similar core values as your own, otherwise it won't be a good fit. You may have heard hiring managers say, "Oh, that person is really good, but I don't think they're a culture fit." When you hear that, they're really saying, "Hey that person is great, but their core values don't match ours."

> *I worked for an organization where my values didn't match theirs. It was a really small company, and as always, I knew nothing about the industry, so the learning curve was a bit steep. I came into work with my usual bright attitude and tried getting to know the people. I was immediately told not to talk because my boss was watching. We were meant to be working and not talking, I guess. (I didn't get that feeling from the interview, so this was news to me.) So, I sat down and started working. It was a strange environment to be in; you could hear a pin drop, it was that quiet!*
>
> *A few months later, I thought, maybe I'll bring some cheer to the place and my boss will lighten up. So, I organized a food drive. I thought that would be a fun way to do something good. I asked my boss and her husband (who was the owner of the company) if I could, and he thought it was a great idea. She reluctantly said yes and made sure to tell me I could only work on the food drive outside*

of work hours. A week later, he proudly brought in so much food, and the look on her face was priceless; she was not happy about it. I don't think it was the fact that we were collecting food for the needy, I think it was because she felt like it was a distraction to work. There were other work practices that tested my ethics too, and when I was vocal with a coworker, **I was fired**. *That was the only job I've ever been fired from. It was such a mismatch to my core beliefs that I just wasn't the right fit for that organization.*

At the end of the day, your core values make up who you are. Looking back at my grandfather and my parents, I can see exactly why I am who I am and where it comes from. My experiences have also taught me what's most important to me, and what I'm willing to tolerate and what I am not. I urge you to think about what's most important to you. What are your non-negotiables? Write them down and keep them in a place where you will always see them to remind yourself what's most important to you, and share them with those closest to you. I keep mine taped to my computer monitor. We'll define your core values in an exercise at the end of Part II.

CHAPTER 5

GET STUFF DONE

Getting things done builds credibility. Building relationships is half of the battle- so you're "in" with the right people. But, how do you stay there? By getting things done, because that means action, which is much more than words. What I'm about to suggest is something that a lot of people already do—it's not an earth-shattering discovery. If you already do these things, you are probably organized and have a great system! If you don't, try these and see if they work for you. Remember that there are a thousand ways to get to the same goal. What works for me may or may not work for you. The most important thing is to build a system that works for you.

My go-to tools are:
- Google or Outlook calendar
- Evernote (some people use OneNote, either one works fine)
- Smartsheet (or any project management system)

I was not paid to promote Evernote, Google, Outlook, or Smartsheet. I'm just a superfan! Use similar tools that you like and work for you! Let's start with your calendar. Here is an example of a fictitious calendar I created in Google:

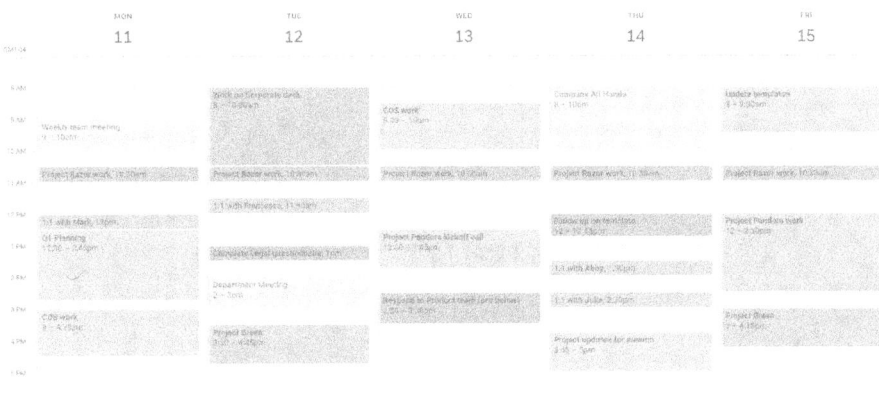

You won't be able to see it in this image, but I color code my calendars. Each related activity is assigned a color. This is so at a glance I can easily see how I'm spending my time. Google is free for anyone to create an account and use. It gives you access to use a suite of tools, including a free calendar. If your company has a paid business version of Google, it's even more informative, because it has advanced insights which actually calculate the percentage of time you're allocating to different tasks based on color.

In addition to color-coding by activity, I also use my calendar to create "meetings" for all those random things I need to get done which I don't want to forget. Like when I'm in a meeting and there's an action item I commit to in the moment, I'll just pick an empty spot and throw it on my calendar. The goal is to move things out of my brain and get it on the calendar, so I never have to think about it again. Of course, you can move it to another day or time if something else comes up, and the beauty of it is that you won't forget about it. This tactic is even great for answering emails or requests. It's a good idea to put context or copy and paste a link to the email or original request like this:

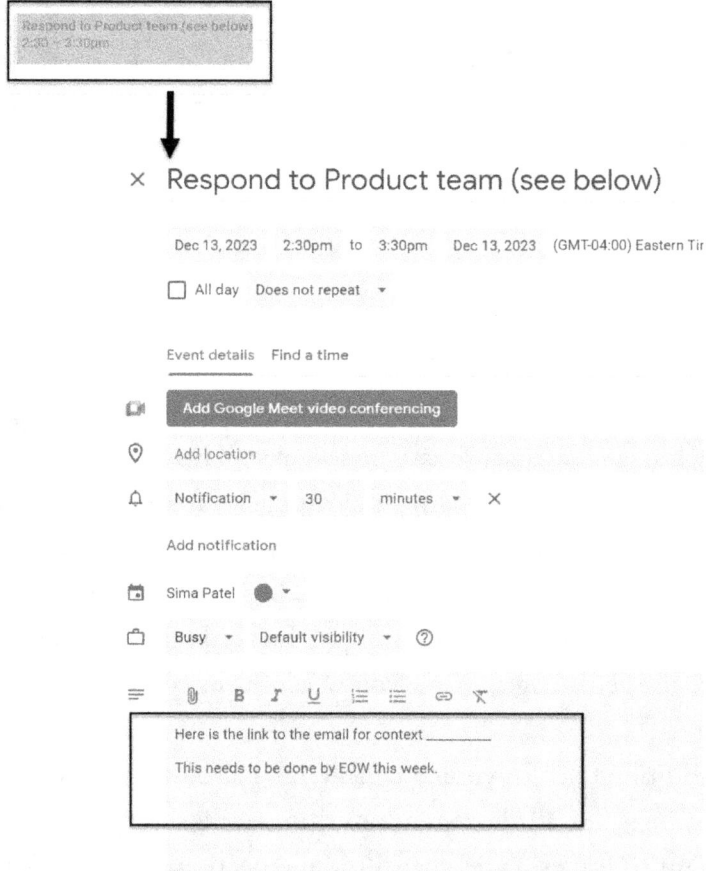

Next, let's talk about note-taking software, such as Evernote. The first thing I'll say about note-taking is that *it's 100 percent necessary*, even if you think you'll remember the information later by memory. Never walk into (or virtually join) a meeting without being ready to take notes. No matter how big or small the meeting is, this is vital. The notes don't have to be formal, just information that makes sense to you. Also, your boss (and others around you) will notice if you're not prepared.

Before I discovered digital notes, I would walk around with a notebook. Flipping through pages trying to find my notes from the last meeting was sometimes challenging. It's not like you can attach a new sheet in between other sheets to keep things organized. Then I discovered Evernote, and it truly changed my life. I would say OneNote or other digital note-taking platforms work similarly, I just use Evernote.

Evernote is a digital note organizer, and it's free to download for up to fifty notes! The paid version has unlimited notes and is reasonably priced. It's so simple, you just open the platform, click on a new note, add a title, and start writing your notes. You can even copy and paste pictures or snippets. It will automatically save as you go. It then saves all your collection of notes and organizes it by most recent. I have hundreds of notes like this, and I use the search bar to find what I'm looking for. This is a great place to add all your training notes (so you can go back anytime and review processes you learned from your people). You can also keep all of your one-on-one notes in here and just keep adding dates. Evernote has saved me so much time because I can instantly find my notes and quickly get up to speed from where I left off during a meeting or when I want to go back to something from months or years ago. I can then just keep adding to that same note. I usually just separate it by date and add in the new information.

Finally, let's talk about project management tools. I may be biased here because I was our company's admin for Smartsheet for a while, but I cannot live without Smartsheet. If you don't have access to a project management tracking tool, you can build something similar in Excel or Google Sheets. The idea is that you keep track of your progress for big tasks or action items you need to accomplish. Using a project tracking system makes it a lot easier to write up reports or updates you might have to provide, and it's really helpful to show how much work you've actually completed. Even if you don't work on official projects, this is still helpful to keep track of your work.

The reason this is so crucial is because it keeps track of all the work you are doing. It's a record of what you've done, what you're doing now, and what you will be doing. Pulling it up during one-on-ones with your manager or even with your team will allow for you to capture quick updates and provide information to your team. It also helps with making justifications for additional resources because you can better articulate all of the tasks associated with the project. I built a project management template; feel free to use this QR code to access it under "Resources" on my site!

These types of organizational tools can help you be sharp, always prepared, and avoid missing a deadline or forgetting to do something. I've described the specific tools that make my life easier so I don't miss a beat. But it's important to find what works best for you, because tools like these are only effective if you use them consistently. Being prepared is so important because it sets the stage for your success. You wouldn't go into a boxing ring without gloves, right? In that same manner, you shouldn't walk into work without the tools you need to survive. In my first job straight out of college, I learned this lesson the hard way.

> *Throughout high school and college, I excelled in school, was a leader, and was generally good at speaking. I was hired as a sales representative for my college newspaper. A year later I moved to the assistant manager position and then was promoted to manager my senior year. When I was hired for my first job, I was chosen out of 500 people who applied. I was at the top of my game, and I don't think I worked that hard to do it. I thought I could easily just fly by the seat of my pants as I had done before. But this company only hired the cream of the crop, and now I was surrounded by people who were (gasp) better than me! I was young and incredibly naive, and I literally came crashing down as I stumbled through my first work presentation to a buyer. Afterward, my boss pulled me aside and asked me how long I had prepared for the presentation.*
>
> *"Prepared? I don't know, maybe a few minutes before we met?"*
>
> *He looked at me and asked what I thought the most important thing I should have done that day was. I told him I should have presented better.*
>
> *He replied, "No, the most important thing you should have done was to prepare for the presentation. The presentation is important, yes. But it's not as important as preparing for it."*

> *I thought a lot about what he said. In previous roles, I could just wing it. But if I wanted to succeed here, I was going to have to start really preparing and anticipating questions and objections..*

Those words have never left me, and I'm glad I learned that lesson so young. I can honestly say there have been times when I have had to wing a presentation, but those times were never as good as the times that I practiced what I was going to say. Take that extra thirty minutes before a big meeting and have everything ready to go, with tabs open and links available. You will be so prepared and feel completely ready. I generally block out thirty minutes on my calendar before something important just to make sure I'm prepared and ready to go. Then, when it's game time, I appear polished, confident, and ready.

So you could have all your ducks in a row, but what about the people you're working with? The agony of waiting on something from someone is enough to drive you crazy! Have you ever sent multiple emails, instant messages, left actual messages, and...well nothing? There is no greater frustration than that. We've all experienced it, here's what I do in those situations that has helped me get answers.

- You need to discuss something important and get feedback/formulate a plan...
  - ▶ Set up a meeting with a clear agenda ahead of time and the action items that need to come out of it. If the meeting is that important to you, send a quick message to make sure your stakeholders will be attending (don't just rely on the accepted invite). This is especially important if it's a recurring meeting. Everyone, including myself, is guilty of skipping a

meeting or two. But, if I know someone is expecting me to be there, there's a higher chance I will show up.
- You asked for that thing so many times and....crickets...
  - I find instant messages are really effective in obtaining an update. I also will copy my manager if I need to (or their manager). But, my last resort and usually effective one is when I will set up a 15 minute meeting with someone and name it "project x sync" (or whatever it is that you need from them). Fifty percent of the time, that person will just go and get the thing done that they should have done in the first place, and then I happily cancel the meeting. The other fifty percent of the time, that person is so busy that they welcome the quick meeting and we knock it out together, or they have questions so they are grateful we can talk through it.

All these tools that I've mentioned come from years of experience, self-reflection, and so much learning and growth. They collectively make me who I am and have built my reputation at work and in life. It appears that I am always on top of my work and that I don't miss a beat, but not because I am just that good. I just rely on my core values to guide me when I'm making decisions. And I use my tools (calendar and notes) to keep me organized so I'm prepared.

There's one last thing I want to mention here, and that is the overwhelming feeling you get when you have SO much in front of you. How do you tackle the big things while the little things keep pouring in? Use all of the tools above. Remember that you have to take one thing at a time. Take the entire project and create a timeline from the finish line all the way to the beginning. When is it due? Start there. Think through all the steps/meetings/etc you need to accomplish what you need to do and build your timeline. All of a sudden, instead of having one big giant project glaring at you, you have much more manageable little tasks to complete. And then it doesn't seem so bad.

CHAPTER 6

DRESS FOR SUCCESS

First impressions matter. You've heard it before, I'm sure, and I know how cliché it sounds, but it's so true! When you dress up, fix your hair, and put on an outfit that fits you well and looks nice, you feel good. Feeling good automatically boosts your confidence, which is your most secret weapon! I'm not talking about spending a lot of money on designer clothes; I definitely don't spend a lot of money on my clothes. But if I'm going into the office, you better believe I'm going to look put together. You might want to dress for the role you want, not the one you have. So pay attention to how formal or casual your work environment is and make your decisions based on that. At the end of the day, the goal is to feel great, and that means putting on what makes you comfortable, confident, and ready to shine!

I worked for a company where, on my first day, I was introduced to a woman who was breathtakingly beautiful. But it wasn't just her beauty that stood out to me. It was that she was dressed so nicely. I had no idea who she was when I first met her. I assumed she was someone important just by the way she carried herself. Turns out, she was a sales director, but I didn't know that at the time. When you dress professionally, people automatically think you're important—it's wild! They give you the respect that you then work hard to earn.

There is someone on my team who always—and I mean always—wears a sport coat and collared shirt with slacks, even on Zoom calls. Sometimes we tease him about it, but I actually think it's pretty great because it shows respect for himself, the people around him, and his work. One time we were in the office, and I was having a meeting with someone from a different department across from the room he was in. Our conference rooms are made of glass so you can see into them. The person I was meeting with glanced across the hall and saw my coworker dressed up as usual.

She didn't know who he was and said, "Wow! Look at that guy—he looks really important. Do you know who he is?"

I laughed and told her who he was. Of course, he is important to our organization, but again, she didn't know that.

You'll notice it's not just in the office. When you dress up and go out, people treat you differently. You stand out and look important. When you dress up and exude confidence, it's just human nature, and we're wired this way. I know the world we live in and the messages we hear tell us it's not how we look that matters, and I agree with that to a certain degree. How you stand out and the first impression you give is what people will remember…and the next impression, and the next, and so it goes as you earn the respect people have visually assigned to you by your behavior.

USE YOUR TOOLS EXERCISE: DISCOVER YOUR CORE VALUES

Here's one way to discover your core values in five steps:

1. Find a quiet place where you can reflect without any distractions. Be well-rested.

2. Get a notebook or use your computer—whatever is most comfortable for you. Write down the most significant moments in your life and why they were important to you. What emotions were you feeling? Consider the times that you were proud or deeply satisfied or even times that you saw someone doing something that you really disagreed with. Why did you feel that way?

   Example:
   My family and I travel to India every few years. We like to buy cases of snacks like chips and cookies. We leave them in the trunk of the car, and every time we pass by families living in tents, we stop by and give snacks to the kids. Their eyes light up with so much joy and excitement, it absolutely warms my heart. The way I feel when I do something for someone else tells me how important it is for me to help others.

3. Reflect on the emotions associated with those moments. If you need help with coming up with a list, you can google a common list of values for inspiration. Aim for five to ten values that really matter to you.

Example:
- Kindness
- Integrity
- Courage
- Accountability
- Honesty

4. Reflect on why each value is so important. Rank your list of values in order of what's *most* important to you (the stuff that's non-negotiable to you and you are willing to fight for).

5. take the top few (there's really no minimum or maximum) and write a statement about why they are so important to you.

Example:
- Help others and be kind. The universe will take care of you, your job is to help others.
- Take 100 percent ownership, whether it's good or bad. Learn to apologize sincerely and do what you say you're going to do.

Place your core values somewhere you will see them regularly. Seeing them so frequently will help validate what you created and keep reminding you what's most important to you as you make decisions. As you grow and evolve, your values may shift, and that's absolutely normal! Try this exercise again from time to time and make changes as you see fit. Important note...if some of the emotions that were most important to you were painful, this is the place to look for your purpose. Our positive emotional experiences help identify our Core Values (character), and our painful emotional experiences help us identify what we are most passionate about, our Purpose and Passion. For example, I'm writing this monograph for people out there who don't know how to navigate their career or stand up for themselves. Everything I learned I stumbled through and made a thousand mistakes. I'm so passionate about helping people because I didn't have blueprints or someone guiding me.

PART III
FIND YOUR VOICE

Have you ever been in a situation where you walked into a room and felt like the *dumbest* person there? It's not that you were dumb or anything, it's more like you felt the people around you were so accomplished and smart. You were really questioning whether you belonged in the same room with the likes of them, breathing the same air. So, you did your best to try to fit in and not say much, all the while freaking out just a little bit inside.

Do you want to know a secret? Every person in that room either feels or has felt that same way. Why is it a secret? Because no one actually talks about it. Everyone wants to appear cool and confident. Impostor syndrome (or what I like to call head trash) literally makes you your own worst enemy. We tend to unknowingly sabotage ourselves. Thoughts of not being good enough, deserving enough, smart enough, or just *enough* for the job are so powerful they drown out the actual facts. And what's in your head is a lot worse than the actual truth. Do you remember graduating from eighth grade and feeling like you were not ready for high school? Or if you went to a university, do you remember leaving the comfort of high school and your hometown? It was scary! Did you think you were ready? Probably not. But looking back, were you? Absolutely. Wherever you are, you've earned your place; you're not there by accident. There's a reason you were invited to the event to rub elbows with accomplished people or were asked to be in that important meeting. You really do belong there.

You know when you're in a meeting and you have a question you really want to ask, but you think about it a thousand times first? How should I word it? Is it a dumb question? What will people think of me? Shouldn't I already know this? Ugh! It's exhausting! So, you wait it out. Someone will ask, right? And then lo and behold, the person you think is the smartest in the room asks the very question you were wondering. And you're like, okay, I'm not dumb.

It works the same in answering questions: you think you have the right answer, but you don't speak up for fear that it's not the right answer and you'll look like an idiot. Then another "smarter" person blurts out the same answer you would have, and they get the glory. Those moments are equally as validating as they are frustrating. So how do you get over impostor syndrome? It's hard. And I mean, *hard*. It's something you have to actively work through all the time. But there are a few things you can do to help keep it at bay and build confidence in your own voice:

1. Give yourself a break (you're NOT supposed to know everything).
2. Remind yourself *every day* why you are so amazing.
3. Have the courage to fight for yourself.

CHAPTER 7

GIVE YOURSELF A BREAK

No one actually knows everything. I know it's a hard concept to believe, but you're not *supposed* to be good at everything. This is an especially hard mindset for people leaders when they have team members who are more experienced in their craft than they are. As a manager, you feel like you should be better or more knowledgeable in your field than your team members are. But in fact, it's actually a really good thing when they're better because your job is to motivate your team and provide the strategy. Their success is ultimately your success, so let them be great at their job and don't be threatened. Remember that your job is to encourage them and create an environment of trust, care, and value so they give their very best.

It's okay to admit you don't know something. Admitting you don't know or understand something doesn't make you weak. It's actually an opportunity to build credibility. First, as I said earlier, no one knows everything, so it's not believable if you pretend you do. Second, if you admit you don't have the answer, tell whoever is asking that you'll get back to them. This is where you leverage that community of people you built and ask them to help you. It could be that you need to learn how something works, or that you need a report, or whatever it might be. When you circle back and provide the answer afterward, it proves that you are reliable. And the next time you say you don't know something, the people around you will be confident that you will find the answer.

Most of the time I don't feel like I know anything. I work in an environment where everyone on my team is an industry expert at what they do. It can be quite intimidating when you're around such highly intelligent and experienced people. Part of my job is to know everything that is happening within my department. I'm in charge of making sure all projects are completed and basically that everything we commit to is executed flawlessly. As a person who has been in so many industries, I don't have the capacity to become an expert in any of them. And that's okay (because I have my people to fall back on), but I do have to know what they're doing and how things work at a high level. So, my go-to phrase to say when I'm learning something really complex (or complex to me, anyway) is to say, "Please talk to me like I'm eight." I say that because an eight-year-old will need to be told information in a very simplistic way that's easy to understand. It makes my job so much easier when someone puts their complex words into simple context. Another benefit to this is that it continues to build a level of trust and deepens the relationship between us, because they see that I actually care about what they're doing.

This works the other way around as well. Sometimes when you push yourself and venture into unknown territory, it's really overwhelming. And while it's so exciting to think about learning new things, it's equally terrifying. You pore over the training materials, read, study, and talk to your network—all the things you're supposed to do. Your brain is full of stuff, and you're still not quite sure if you know it. Here's what you do;

find someone who knows nothing about what you're learning and ask them to listen as you explain it. If, after you're done, they understand what you are saying, you really do know your stuff.

I can't recall how many times I thought I didn't know what I was talking about until I tried to explain to my family. First, I would explain it to my husband and then simplify it even more to my kids. If they got the gist of what I was saying, then I was good. It's easy to memorize things, but if you can take information in and learn to distill it down so "regular" people understand it, you're in a good place! Our brain is the most complex and amazing organ in our bodies, it creates clarity when we speak out loud to others (or ourselves) what we think and feel.

Another thing that kills confidence is making mistakes. Ugh, it's the worst, right? I always laugh when people say, "Oh, I hate making mistakes." Like, duh. Doesn't everyone? No one—and I mean absolutely no one—wakes up in the morning and says, "Hey! I think I'll make some mistakes today!" It's called a mistake because it's made accidentally with no ill intention. But the moment you realize you made a mistake is the moment you have to take accountability and work with your manager on a solution. I get it, though; it's *hard* to admit when you make a mistake. You don't want to come across as incompetent, and you certainly don't want to cause a domino effect of something bad either. Trust me, sooner or later you will make a mistake, and your mistake (no matter how bad it is) won't matter as much as *how you handle it*. This kind of goes back to core values. If accountability and honesty are important to you, you'll do the right thing and admit your mistake.

I was a manager once leading a five-person sales team and eight operations people, new to the organization, and fairly new in leadership. The previous manager conducted unethical behavior and pretty much was absent from the center. The team just kind of did whatever they wanted. They were really smart and capable, but with no leadership, it was more like a fun place to hang out than somewhere actual work was happening. The center was also notorious for not passing audits and just generally being a bit of a mess. I had a plan: I was going to exercise discipline, implement my changes, and we were going to get back on track really quick! I came in guns blazing, ready to conquer the office and get everyone in gear.

Oh, did that backfire on me. They hated me, and when I say hated, I mean they really, really did not like me, not even a little bit. I would hear them talking about me from my office. They would whisper about me as I walked by, and all my requests were met with reluctant execution. I remember sitting in my car and crying. I called my boss and told him what was going on. I told him I wasn't cut out to fix the center and that I didn't think I could do it. My boss was kind and patient with me, and he told me that I could do two things. I could either walk away, or I could use this as a learning opportunity to stop and get to know my team and learn from them.

I went home that day with my confidence completely shot. I really wanted to give up; like, how embarrassing is it to go back knowing they pretty much ran me out of the office? I thought a lot about what happened. What did I do to deserve their treatment? Didn't they know my intention? Hmmm...well, actually, no they really didn't, did they? They just saw me as another person walking in that door trying to "set them straight." I didn't take the time to get to know them, to understand their concerns, or really get to the root of why everything got so out of hand. My team didn't feel listened to or understood in any way. I just started "managing" rather than leading. I really messed it up, and I was mortified. As painful as it was for me, I decided to be brave and go back. I think they were shocked to see me walk through the door.

I called a meeting, and I apologized for coming in so strong, and admitted all my shortcomings to them. Instantly, their glances softened toward me. There I was, humbly asking for forgiveness and still feeling embarrassed with my confidence out the door. It took time, but I earned their trust, and we really became a team together. We turned the center around and started performing much better. When I ended up leaving the company to pursue other opportunities, my team snuck in and worked at night to throw me a surprise party the next day. They didn't have to do this, but they did. I am so grateful to my manager for giving me grace and encouraging me to face my fears. This story was so pivotal in teaching me humility and keeps me humble today.

CHAPTER 8

REMIND YOURSELF EVERY DAY WHY YOU ARE SO AMAZING

Close your eyes and think about all the things you have accomplished in your life. And I do mean life, not just work. You play many roles (wear many hats) and influence far more than you realize. There are so many people who look up to you, depend on you, and are so proud of you! I'm here to tell you it's okay—no, it's actually crucial—to recognize your accomplishments and be proud of them. We live in this society where we're not supposed to brag about ourselves as if talking about success is taboo. Why, though? I get that you shouldn't brag about money or all the materialistic things you might have (that would make you kind of a jerk). But you absolutely should be proud of all you have done despite many challenges along the way.

If you don't celebrate the little wins in life, you'll lose yourself in waiting for the big wins. Treat yourself like a million bucks and you'll *feel* like a million bucks! Every morning, look at yourself in the mirror and tell yourself how amazing you are. Talk about the awesome things you're going to do today and the people around you who will be impacted by your contribution. The more you *say it out loud*, the more clear it becomes, and the more you will believe it! If you like to write things down, I also suggest journaling. It's nice to look back on your life and see the progress you've made. Don't underestimate the value you bring to others and how you impact them every day. I know all of this is so much easier said than done. We've been programmed to do and feel the opposite of all this, so it's that much harder to break the barrier. Because it's so hard, you have to surround yourself with people who will encourage you and remind you every day how amazing and inspirational you are.

We all need a nudge sometimes. Pep talks, reminders, and words of encouragement go a really long way and can help us make decisions that could be life-changing. Looking back on your life, do you regret not taking the chance or pushing yourself in a moment that could have been triumphant?

> *I was invited to a meeting filled with powerhouse executives from Fortune 500 companies. I was really excited to attend, but I definitely didn't feel like I belonged there. I had the option of joining the meeting virtually or in person. Up until the night before the meeting, I was going to attend the meeting virtually (safe, right?). My daughter was aware of my big meeting and assumed I would attend in person. She was shocked to learn I was nervous and wanted to hide behind my computer. She looked me in the eye and reminded me how smart and amazing I was, that I earned my way there, and I shouldn't give up the opportunity to be in the same room as the accomplished people I looked up to. If I didn't take a chance on myself and be there with confidence, I would regret it because*

opportunities don't present themselves a second time. She was right, and I couldn't believe I almost didn't show up.

The next day, I took a deep breath, had all my materials prepared in case I needed to speak up in the meeting, and I showed up, dressed for success. Two things happened in that meeting.

1. I got to meet some very important people and hear their questions and thought processes.

I felt validated knowing that some of the things they were saying were things I was thinking as well.

2. I will never forget how I felt sitting in that meeting. I was proud that I allowed myself to be uncomfortable, and I built my confidence a bit more by being validated that my thoughts weren't that far off from people who I thought were so much better than me.

In those moments of doubt, surround yourself with the right people. Find the people who will lift you up. Lean on the people who won't let you take the easy way out. Learn from the people who will make you better. And listen to people who truly believe in you. I promise, you will never regret taking a chance on yourself. Thank you Meera.

CHAPTER 9

HAVE THE COURAGE TO FIGHT FOR YOURSELF

How many times did you miss an opportunity to do something? It was there, staring at you in the face, and you thought about it over and over again, but you just couldn't bring yourself to do it. Those are the worst regrets! In other words, every time you don't stand up for yourself, sit on the sideline instead of speaking up, sell yourself short, or don't ask for what you want is a time you will not get it. You know this, and I know this, so why is it so hard to do? Because we're taught to be polite and not ask for what we need. I'm not sure when it became polite to not ask for what we need, and maybe it is still looked at as crass, but damn. It's time to change that stigma, isn't it?

Shout out to all my people pleasers out there—you know who you are! I'm right there with you! It's almost impossible to ask for something because you don't want to disappoint someone, hurt their feelings, or seem ungrateful. But here's the honest truth: no one will ever not respect you for standing up for yourself and asking for what you deserve. Even if in the end you didn't get exactly what you wanted, at least you know you stood up for yourself and tried. Looking someone clearly in the eyes and telling them what you need, politely, but firmly, will earn you so much respect. You'll be surprised to learn that people don't automatically just know what you want (even if you hint at it). You may be lucky and have an amazing leader who is proactively looking for ways to groom and grow you, handing you new assignments and promotions without you asking. Those leaders are few and far between. Most of the time, they're not doing it on purpose, they simply have no idea what you really want. So, it's up to you. Have the courage to fight for yourself and have that difficult conversation.

I was new in an organization once. I really liked my manager! She was smart, a really hard worker, and very well respected in our organization. Everyone knew and liked her; she had an amazing reputation of being a great leader. I felt very lucky to be hired by her and was eager to learn from her. About three months into my role, my manager let me know we would be going through a reorganization and, although I would still be on her team, I would be reporting to someone else (who was newly hired onto our team due to an acquisition). I understood that change is constant, and although I felt disappointed that I wouldn't get that one-on-one time with her anymore, I would make it work.

Then I met him. He looked like a scared rabbit, like I was going to chew him up and spit him out. I gave him a chance, though; I prepared for our meeting, asked him questions to get to know him and his leadership style, and inquired about the plans he had for our team. I could instantly see he was inexperienced and was sort of thrown into the position. I walked away really frustrated, not because I thought I was better than him, but because I knew I was no longer going to learn as much or be challenged. I was going to give to the company, but the company wasn't going to give back to me.

I went home that night and really thought about it. I chose to work at this company expecting to learn a great deal and grow within the organization. I didn't see my new manager as someone who would be my advocate or really teach me. So, I emailed my original manager and very kindly asked her to carefully consider if this person was the right fit to be my leader. I trusted her judgment, and I knew he could have just been nervous that day and made a bad impression, but I asked her to really consider my goals and how I'd thrived since I started there. If she honestly felt that he would be the best fit to continue to challenge and push me to be better, I would happily accept the change and do my very best. However, if she felt that he might not be the best fit, I asked her to please reconsider continuing to be my manager.

I closed my eyes and hit send. It was agonizing; I couldn't believe I sent that email. I almost regretted it once it was sent. She could have really read that as me being arrogant. And I could see how it could come across like that, but I needed someone who would make me better, and I wasn't convinced it was him.

The next day she responded. She told me she appreciated my honesty and respected my approach in fighting for myself and decided it would be best for her to continue being my manager. I took a chance and stood up for myself. I got what I wanted. This situation strengthened our relationship, and she probably respected me so much more because of it.

I once came out of a really rough work situation. I was damaged, and my confidence was completely shattered. I really had to dig deep to remember who I was and what I had already accomplished to get to where I wanted to be. I know I mentioned this story before, but obtaining my PMP certification was a turning point for me. I knew that if I did that, I could do anything. I started to regain my confidence, and then I met one of the smartest women I have ever known in my life. She carried herself with such confidence, and she was not only an incredible strategist, but could execute flawlessly. She told me she thought I was all those things too, and gave me a lotus bracelet to remind myself of how strong and smart I am. I wore that bracelet every day, and each time I looked at it, it was a reminder to me that I really was all of those things. That bracelet helped me get through some challenging times. I'm so grateful to her.

I'll be honest. As I said earlier, battling impostor syndrome is really hard. It's a constant work in progress, but understanding yourself and practicing these steps can help you shift your mindset and reduce imposter syndrome feelings. By the time you get to your more difficult goals, you'll feel ready to take them on! Every time you start feeling like you can't do something or you don't belong somewhere, think back to that achievement list you made. As I mentioned before, imposter syndrome will never fully go away, and it probably shouldn't - so you stay humble. Impostor syndrome is a complete mindset. Henry Ford said in the September 1947 issue of Reader's Digest, "Whether you think you can, or you think you can't–you're right."

Imposter Syndrome is such a complex thing. You might have no idea where it's coming from, and journaling can help uncover its roots. Do you subtly or subconsciously diminish yourself because of your childhood? Your cultural upbringing? Being bullied when you were younger?

Find the roots, pull them out, and replace them with affirmations that are true, noble, pure, right, and your absolute best self.

> *My imposter syndrome manifested itself from several sources. I had an amazing childhood, but I am the youngest in my whole family (that includes siblings and cousins from both sides of the family). I think people always looked at my older sister as the cool, confident, capable one in all aspects. I always felt like that kid who could never quite compare to her - and - while it's not the case anymore, I've still tried to prove that I'm more than that to everyone around me. It took me a lot of years to realize I was really just competing with myself. No one sees me that way, in fact they see me as cool, confident, successful, and all the things I thought I wasn't. Isn't it crazy how the version we think others see isn't reality at all?*

Impostor syndrome is something that you have to work at every day. I don't think it ever totally goes away, and that's actually not a bad thing. Aiming for 80 percent confidence with 20 percent impostor syndrome will keep you confident enough while being humble and on your toes at all times. Confidence comes with experience and learning, and it requires so much courage. Chances are, you're not going to come out of the gate feeling confident all of the time. The more experience you have and the more mistakes you've learned from, the easier it will be to drown out the negative thoughts in your head. You have to be surrounded by people who will pick you up and remind you how amazing you are, even when you fall down. And you have to allow yourself to make mistakes and learn from them. No one just knows things; everyone learns things either from others or their own experiences. You are competing with yourself, and the battle you are fighting is with you alone.

On my first day at work many years ago, a vice president of sales came to greet us, and she told us this story:

Imagine you buy your first home, and you're so excited about it! It's amazing, it's perfect, it's...wait. How did we not see this ugly 1970s yellow-green and brown flowery wallpaper? What?! Immediately, you say very loudly that you refuse to put up any pictures in this house until that wallpaper is off and it's been repainted with a more appropriate shade to match the rest of the house. You proceed to move in the rest of the boxes, and you stare at that atrocity on the wall with despair. You will take care of that as soon as you unpack. And then you unpack, and it's still looking back at you with its yellow-green and brownness. You vow you will change it next month, because you're traveling this month and next is just around the corner, right? Three months go by. You know you need to get to it, but you're so busy with the kids starting school. For sure, once they're back in school it will be easier! Now it's winter. It doesn't look so yellow-green and brown anymore. Ugh, it's fine, you'll do it next year.

So, as you can guess, the wallpaper never does get changed. The metaphor here is that when you're new you see things so much more clearly than people who have been in that organization or their role for a long time. You have a fresh perspective, new ideas, and a whole different way of seeing something. The wallpaper is ugly, not something you're used to. So, I implore you to never stop seeing *how* ugly the wallpaper is. Be that squeaky wheel. Say the words and don't stop, because you're probably right and that change you suggest might be the thing that actually works.

FIND YOUR VOICE EXERCISE: KILL IMPOSTER SYNDROME

The idea of this exercise is to start small. It's the little wins that give us the confidence to keep going for more. Think of it as crawling first, then walking, and then running. The more wins you have, the more you will feel capable and be able to fight off feelings of impostor syndrome.

Build Your Achievement List

1. Find a quiet place where you can reflect. Think back on your school years or career. Make a list of all of your achievements (or as many as you remember), big and small. These could be academic, work, or life related.

   Example:
   - Beat out 500 people for a job
   - Got a 3.8 GPA while working in college
   - Climbed two mountains in one day

2. Next to each accomplishment, write down your skills, qualities, or efforts that contributed to your success.

   Example:
   - Beat out 500 people for a job: prepared for interview, practiced speaking, really wanted the job (Tenacious)
   - Got a 3.8 GPA while working in college: studied, practiced good time management, prioritized, consistently worked hard, didn't give up (Disciplined)

- Climbed two mountains in one day: didn't give up, kept telling myself I could keep going just a little longer (Overcomer)

3. Look carefully at what you've written down and reflect on all of the things you accomplished. What did you do to achieve those victories? How did you *feel* when you reached those accomplishments? Do you see patterns or recurring strengths that have played a role in multiple achievements?

    Example:
    - I took the time to prepare
    - I didn't give up
    - I was consistent

    I was so proud of myself in all those moments because I really earned my place there. I worked hard, didn't give up, was consistent with my quality of work, and was always prepared. As long as I continue doing those things, I can do anything!

Build Your Goal List

4. Now make a separate list of all the things you want to do in your life or at work. It can be a brain dump of big things or small things, just all of it.

    Example:
    - Expand my scope and footprint at work
    - Sharpen my presentation skills
    - Become an expert in my job
    - Get a certification

5. Categorize and group that list by level of difficulty
   - Level 1 = easy to do, requires little effort
   - Level 2 = a little harder, requires some effort
   - Level 3 = difficult, requires major effort

   Example:
   - Expand my scope and footprint at work: 1
   - Get a certification: 3
   - Sharpen my presentation skills: 1
   - Become an expert in my job: 2

6. Make a plan with actionable goals to start with the level 1 tasks. Use your calendar and put the steps in as action items to do. If you need to, set recurring events. You don't have to do *all* the things on your list. Start out doing something that you can easily do and work your way there. Set a realistic expectation for yourself. Everyone has different resources and situations. Remember that you're not competing with anyone other than yourself.

   Example:
   For the first half of this year, I have four goals:
   - Expand my scope and footprint at work: 1
     - Speak up more in meetings (start at the next team meeting).
     - Tap into my people to learn more about the areas where my work crosses over with another team.
     - Ask for more responsibilities.
     - Network and set up meetings (go back to the organizational chart if needed).

- Sharpen my presentation skills: 1
  - ▶ Take an online speaking class (block practice time into my calendar).
  - ▶ Ask for a presentation opportunity. Start small with my internal team.
- Become an expert in my job: 1
  - ▶ Study outside of my role to learn more about the industry and how it works.
  - ▶ Subscribe to blogs and articles that pertain to my work.
  - ▶ Look for learning opportunities like seminars or events I can attend.

Execute and Reflect

7. Before you execute the action items to reach each of your level 1 goals, read through your achievement list. This will help remind you why you *will* succeed in what you are setting out to do.

8. Now you just have to start! Sometimes it's a little hard to start, but once you get going, it's so much easier.

9. As you begin completing your level 1 goals, you will gain confidence in yourself with each one. Remember that building confidence takes time, so be patient with yourself. Start a journal and begin writing down how you're feeling as you conquer your goals in small steps.

Rinse and Repeat

10. Once you've achieved your easy, low-hanging fruit goals, step up to the next level of goals and repeat the process.

Shout It Out!

11. Share your success with that circle of yours who will be thrilled for you and proud of you. We *need* to hear positive affirmations all the time, no matter how great we are. Rewarding and celebrating will accelerate the Rinse and Repeat cycle!!!

12. Do you ever look back at an object or picture from your childhood and find it brings you right back there? You can remember everything—the smell, the feel, and the way it looked. Our brains are really good at taking us back in time when we come in contact with memorable items. So, use this to your advantage. When you accomplish something big, buy yourself a piece of jewelry, or something to put on your desk that you see all of the time. Think about your journey as you put that bracelet on or place the paperweight on your desk. It's a symbol of everything you did and how good it made you feel. The next time you are feeling like you can't do something. Look at your symbolic object and remember what you did. If you could do that, you can do this! You'll notice that I use a lotus symbol for this section because that's my power symbol. As I mentioned earlier in this chapter, the lotus bracelet my friend gave me was everything I needed to remind me what I had inside of me all along.

CONCLUSION

I started this book with my grandfather's story, and I am ending it with my parents' story. I learned I inherited my altruistic tendencies from my grandfather and my tenacity and gumption from my parents. The idea of never giving up, fighting for what I want, being efficient, having courage, and taking risks are all traits I inherited naturally from my mom and dad and learned as they demonstrated to me.

> *My parents, Bachu and Hansa Hajari, immigrated to the U.S. and settled in San Francisco in 1970. My parents had no knowledge of American culture. Like most immigrants, they had very little money ($16.00 to be exact, which would be worth $126.49 by today's standards). They settled in the very sketchy Tenderloin district of San Francisco and began their lives.*
>
> *My mom barely spoke English, and my dad, although he had a degree in chemistry, couldn't find a job in his area of study. Discrimination made it impossible for either of them to get a good job. So, they basically had to start over, working any entry-level jobs they could find. My dad got a job working for someone who owned over twenty restaurants across the Bay Area. He would wake up in the wee hours of the morning and start his day by doing odd jobs in various restaurants. When I say odd, I mean he would cut onions for four hours straight. Could you imagine that? Working eighteen hours a day, he would trudge home and start all over again the next day.*

Life was so hard for them and much different from what they imagined the American Dream to be. There were nights my parents didn't eat because there was no food. My dad would come home from work to find my mom asleep already because she couldn't face her tired and hungry husband. She would leave a bowl over the stove to indicate there was no food that night.

He had one really good thing going for him, though: he was tenacious, and he was a quick learner. He was working as a dishwasher one day when one of the cooks didn't show up to work. Being brave and knowing he had nothing to lose, he asked his boss if he could step in. His boss laughed and thought it would be entertaining to let my dad try. So, he did. What his boss didn't know was my dad had been watching the cooks and taking mental notes. He knew he could do the job and he would make more money if he was a cook. Lo and behold, he did really well as a cook that day. So, his boss had to eat his words and give him a position as a cook.

Six months later, the head chef showed up to work very drunk. My dad marched up to his boss and said he'd been watching the head chef and knew how to run the kitchen. His manager decided to give him a try, as he had no other choice that day. My dad ran that kitchen like a boss. His leadership style and attention to detail were impeccable. Wouldn't you know it, he took over as the head chef at the restaurant.

My mom applied at many retail stores, but not being able to speak English really worked against her. She never gave up, though, and one day she did get a job working in a candy store. My mom learned later that she got the job because the owner thought she had an honest face. She was so grateful and such a hard worker. When she was working, my mom ran the store by herself. On her days off, the store required two people to produce the same output as she did on her own. Working on Fisherman's Wharf drew in a lot of tourists, and my mom learned English quickly.

She unexpectedly got pregnant with my sister. They couldn't afford to keep her and work at the same time, so when my sister was a year old, my grandparents came and picked her up and took her to India, where they raised her for the next few years. It was probably the hardest thing my parents had ever done to let their only daughter at that time go. It was also probably the best motivation, knowing the faster they saved money, the faster they could bring her back home.

The two of them worked really hard for the next four years. They saved enough money to leave San Francisco and buy a small ten-room motel in Portland, Oregon. My parents picked up my sister and brought her home, and they had me a few years later.

I can't imagine how difficult it must have been to live through all of that. It's not just them; all immigrants have a similar story. They had the courage to fight for themselves and their families. **When you have nothing to lose and everything to gain, you take more risks and do whatever you need to survive.** *I am so incredibly proud of both of them, and their silent voices are always in my heart and in my head. There were so many moments in my life that I wanted to take the easy way out or I was scared to do something. And then I remembered what they did, and I could hear my dad telling me "You can do anything you want. You just have to work hard and have determination and enthusiasm for what you're doing." My mom was so nurturing and taught me how to be soft and show affection. She would always tell me how important it is to*

> *be efficient with my time. After all, we're all given the same amount of time in a day; it's what we do with it that really matters. They are now very happily retired and in their early eighties.*

It's not just my parents I've learned lessons from; I have learned from my family, friends, colleagues, and managers. I've received a little piece of something from everyone I've met. If I could sum up the biggest lessons, they would be:

- I'm not supposed to know everything.
- Nothing great comes from me sitting on the sidelines.
- The most profound learning I ever had was born from disaster.
- Forgiving myself for my mistakes allowed me to move on and grow.
- Listen to other people's stories, especially those who are older and more experienced.
- Surround myself with the right people. I need people in my life who remind me that I can do things when I can't remind myself.
- If I'm ever in a place where I don't know what to do, I should rely on my core values to guide me.
- Never stop giving to others.

Being in my forties has really validated one thing for me: it's the journey that matters, not the ending. The journey will teach you so many lessons; no matter how much advice you get (and yes, I see the irony, because all I've done in these pages is give advice), you have to live your life and make your own mistakes. Your people are there to guide and motivate you. Your tools are there to help you succeed so you can gain the confidence in your own voice to come out as a winner on the other side.

If you think this book has helped you and it might help someone else, feel free to share this QR code:

ACKNOWLEDGMENTS

It takes a village to get you through life, especially at work. Stop for a second and think. Who were people in your life who helped you? And I don't mean the ones who just cheered you on. I'm also talking about those people who challenged you, offered you critical feedback (that you maybe didn't want but *needed* to hear), or put aside their priorities to help you along the way. Do their faces come to mind? Have you ever truly thanked them? It could be the smallest moments with the biggest impact. My monograph is *full* of people I learned from along the way. Some made me cry, and that's okay; I needed to grow up. Others built my confidence, and everyone in between played a role in my growth throughout my career and life. So, it's incredibly important for me to thank them.

My first thank you is to God without whom I would be nothing without. My life starts and ends there.

To my **Mota** and **Ba** (grandfather and grandmother), thank you for starting our family legacy; we have so much to live up to and be proud of. I hope this book lives on so no one forgets the beautiful work you've put forth into this world that positively changes thousands of lives each year.

Anyone that knows me knows how much my family means to me. I am most proud and thankful to my parents who taught us the bond of family and what it means to sacrifice for one another. Hugging and saying "I love you" was such a staple in my family. We always showed each other how much we cared, and that got passed down to me and my sister. We each have our own families that emulate the same kind of bond. I truly thank my mom for that. I was also lucky to have the kind of dad who took me to Disneyland when I was seven (just the two of us, it was incredible). He encouraged me to push myself and be brave. He was so affectionate and gentle yet so incredibly strong. He never let anything get in his way, even his crazy harebrained ideas sometimes. There will never be two people like my parents, **Bachu & Hansa Hajari**. I owe everything I am to the two of them.

To my husband of twenty-one years, **Nayan Patel**, I am so lucky to have such a supportive partner by my side. You have given me so much encouragement, support, and love. You've always believed in me, even when I didn't believe in myself. I am so grateful for you and the life we have built together.

To my daughter, **Meera Patel**, you are everything I wanted to be at your age. Your maturity, wisdom, intelligence, self-respect, and confidence are extraordinary. The discipline you have shown in your business, Lipology, is incredibly inspiring. Keep on shining, you will go so far!

To my son, **Ronak Patel**, never have I ever met anyone with such a big heart. You are brave, smart, so creative, and tenacious. You never let anything stand in your way and your thirst for knowledge is such a beautiful thing. I see so much of myself in you. I can't wait to see what you do in life.

To my sister, **Sneha Kana**, my best friend, I literally can't breathe without you. You are the real rock (and President) of our family and the most loyal person I know. I've learned so much from you.

To my brother-in-law, **Balvant Kana**, you really are my second dad. The one I want to always make proud. In those moments in life when I'm not sure what path to take, I think of what you would do. You have always taught me to do the right thing.

To my niece, **Neelam Kana**, aka my "first born" I cannot begin to tell you how much you have taught me. Your bravery, ambition, integrity, and grace is truly inspiring. The world is your oyster!

To my nephew, **Avin Kana**, your fanatic discipline sets the highest standards for all of those around you. You are truly kind, honest, and give your whole heart in everything you do.

To my other sisters, fate made us family, and I couldn't be happier. Thank you both for always supporting and encouraging me. **Hemina Patel**, your journey is the most inspiring I've ever witnessed. You've let nothing stand in your way, despite obstacles that have found you. **Preeti Patel**, it's been such a joy to watch you find your confidence and excel in your career. **Anika Patel**, thank you so much for the many edits in this book. You are brilliant and have so much to offer this world; you have such a bright future! Thank you also to my mother-in-law, **Nirmalaben**, and my late father-in-law, **Mohanbhai**.

While my family at home has been my foundation, my families at work have been equally important in my journey. They deserve so much gratitude, so thank you very much from the bottom of my heart.

Coach Keith Cupp, this monograph would not be possible without you. You are kind, humble, and so brilliant. I cannot begin to thank you enough for teaching me how to be a leader and exposing me to some of the most incredible coaches in the world. You are the greatest coach I know, and I'm lucky to have met you.

Coach Mike Mirau, your heart is as big as your state! You pushed me when I needed it the most, and for that I will always be grateful. Thank you for being there for me.

Coach Mike Goldman, thank you for advising me to not wait five years to write this. Watching your success in coaching and as an author and speaker is truly inspiring!

Abby Drago-Berg, I have no words to thank you for all that you have done for me. You have been my best and most harmonious partner at work and I appreciate your sound advice and friendship for all these years. I admire you so much, and you have pushed me to grow in so many ways.

McKayla Gallup, you are probably one of the most brilliant, resilient, and kindest people I have ever hired. If there was ever a true definition of an "A" player- you, are it. Thank you for being by my side as we tackled every obstacle together. I hope I get the pleasure of working with you in the future, but my guess is I will be working for you one day!

Francesca Lubbok, I admire you so much! You are one of the most intelligent, inspiring, unbelievably amazing people I know. Thank you for the lotus bracelet; it has served its purpose for me more than you will ever know.

Bubba Nunnery, you are not only my co-worker, but have become a very dear friend! You have been and will continue to be my sounding board. I admire your wit, humor, and ability to command the entire room with your infectious personality.

Shawn Thornhill, I am so incredibly proud to have been able to watch you grow into an amazing leader. Your willingness to learn and grow, your hard work, and positive attitude will get you so far!

Mark Sapiano, there is no one quite like you! You brought something so special to our team, and I will miss you tremendously. I hope you enjoy your much deserved retirement. Thank you for always making my job easier- I appreciate you so much!

Al Raymond, your voice of reason always rings in my ear. Your humor and immense vocabulary are so appreciated! I love working with you!

Simon McDougall, you are the most incredible leader I have ever had the privilege of serving. I truly thank you for seeing the best in me, pushing me when I needed it, and so flawlessly showing everyone around you that such an important person can be so down to earth. You have every quality a great leader should. Thank you for everything.

Henry Schuck, thank you for building the kind of organization that made me want to do everything in my power to join. Your authenticity, passion, kindness, and compassion for your people and your customers is truly remarkable. And the fact that you built this incredible business from the ground up is so inspiring.

Samantha Montgomery, you always put the needs of your people before your own. Thank you for always having my back and giving me opportunities to shine.

Mark Johnson, thank you so much for taking a chance on me. You have no idea how much I needed it. You always had my back and protected me and those around you, I respect and admire you so much.

Chris Hays, thank you for giving me grace and a chance to fix what I broke. You could have really been hard on me, but instead you lead with empathy and I really appreciate it.

Natasha Azar, thank you for reminding me that life gives you certain moments for certain reasons and to appreciate them and use them.

Sailaxmi Malkarnekar, thank you for teaching me how to run projects the right way. You are the greatest program manager I know.

Rachel Stone, I appreciate the partnership you have always displayed. No matter how difficult a situation, you come to my rescue and work with me- even when that means editing this book for me at the last minute.

Keith Rofinot, thank you for being an amazing partner as we tackled the Northern Oregon territory. You taught me how to be firm and hold people accountable.

Mike Burns, thank you for being so kind and letting me down gently, and giving me support when I needed it the most.

Debbie Walery and **Denice Williams**, you are two of the classiest (best dressed) women I know. Thank you, Debbie, for being my mentor, and thank you both for emulating leadership with such grace.

Hallie Dozier, you are a powerhouse of a woman. No one commands a room with such confidence like you do. I remember the first time I met you, I walked away thinking how much I wanted to be just like you (still do)!

Sean O'Brien, thank you for teaching me to face my fears and reflect on my mistakes. You also taught me how to take something really complex and simplify it. That concept and method has helped me tremendously in my career.

Ryan Pansini, you were my first manager straight out of college. Thank you for teaching me the importance of being prepared at all times, and holding me accountable when I needed it. I still think of you everytime I hear Eminem sing "Lose Yourself," as you would so often tell me that I only have one shot to make that impression and the sale.

To all of these amazing individuals I've named above, and those that I'm sure I've missed along the way, I hope you see the size of impact your small gestures made. I hope you keep doing what you're doing because what you might think is an insignificant piece of advice, or coaching can profoundly shape someone's life. It could even throw them onto a completely different and amazing trajectory than they ever thought possible. In addition to giving amazing advice to your mentees, tell them about mistakes you've made and lessons you've learned. Remember that when they look at you, they only see your accomplishments. They don't see all of the scars that you have from every situation you faced in the past. They need to know it's okay to make mistakes and that they too will reach their definition of success.

To those on the receiving end of kindness, make it a point to thank the people who make even the smallest difference in your life. You have no idea what a token of appreciation does. It creates a trickle-down effect: it's validating and reinforces people to share the love. They will then be reminded to thank someone in their life. Small acts create massive waves. And you'll never regret making someone's day.

One last request I have of my female readers is to be kind to other women. It's *hard enough* competing in this world in finding our equality. We have to be shining examples of how women must build each other up and support one another. Let's stop fighting each other, and instead cheer one another on! Our daughters *need* to see how we positively treat each other, it will strengthen their character and allow them to build confidence. **The best gift we can give our daughters is the ability to not think twice about advocating for themselves, to be 100% confident that their voice will be heard, and to fly high because the ceiling was already shattered.** I don't know if we're there yet, but it feels like we're getting closer with each generation. I want to honor my daughter Meera Patel for being a constant reminder of what I'm fighting for.

During the height of the pandemic, at the age of eleven years old, Meera came to me as I was busy working remotely and we were all stuck at home. She stood in front of me as I was typing away at my computer and proudly declared she was going to start a business. Now as any mother would- I didn't really take her seriously and asked her what she was going to sell. She proceeded to tell me she's been working on making homemade lip scrubs.

I stopped what I was doing because clearly, she had given this some thought. Meera was very much (and still is) into proper skin care and she always had chapped lips. I asked her to bring me some of her scrub, and I tried it. I was actually surprised- it was good. Now I was interested. I put my business coach hat on and started grilling her a bit. I asked her how her product would be different from other products, how much does it cost to make, how much will she charge, where will she sell it, etc.

Some of the answers she had and others she said she would get back to me. I told her I would fully support and guide her, but the work would 100% be on her. Meera agreed and began her market research. She gave out samples, asked many different people what flavors and colors they liked and came to the conclusion that she found some sort of correlation between what people liked and their astrological sign. That was it. Lipology was born.

Each lip scrub has a different flavor and color, each appealing to an astrological sign- 12 different flavors for each of the zodiac. She got to work quickly and created each product doing research on food safety and rules and regulations. Meera then built her website and learned how to use a credit card reader. She started selling her product online and at farmers markets. To date she's sold over 500 units and counting. In addition to that, Meera was the youngest member of the Vancouver Chamber of Commerce in Vancouver, WA and is now the youngest member of the East Cobb Chamber of Commerce in the Atlanta area.

My girl's dream is to be a CEO one day, I think she's kind of already there. I am so incredibly proud of her and her accomplishments. It's now four years later and she's still working hard at her business. Meera has aspirations of achieving her undergrad and going on to get her MBA. I can't wait to see what she does next! Here is her website if you want more information:

MY FAVORITE LEADERSHIP BOOKS

Anyone who knows me knows I love reading! In addition to all of the people in my life that I've learned from, these books have had a similar impact on me. There are so many nuggets of amazing information in books. It was hard to choose favorites because there are so many more that should be included in this list. But, here are my top picks, in no particular order. Some may appeal to you over others. Read what catches your eye and keep the theory of throwing all the advice onto your plate and digesting what you like!

Finding your people, building relationships and learning to be a leader:
- Getting Naked by Patrick Lencioni
- Never Lose a Customer Again by Joey Coleman
- Multipliers by Liz Wiseman
- The Five Dysfunctions of a Team by Patrick Lencioni
- The Book of Relationship Building: Understanding People, Building Rapport, and Meaningful Connections by Scott D Snell

Finding and using your tools
- Atomic Habits by James Clear
- Crucial Conversations by Joseph Grenny, Kerry Patterson Ron McMillan, Al Switzler, and Emily Gregory
- Mastering Productivity in Today's Fast-Paced Office: Boost Your Efficiency and Achieve Success in the Modern Workplace with Expert Productivity Strategies by Laurel .S Cousins
- The 7 Habits of Highly Effective People by Stephen R. Covey

Finding your voice and taking care of yourself:
- Year of YES: How to Dance It Out, Stand in the Sun and Be Your Own Person by Shonda Rhimes
- Your Oxygen Mask First by Kevin Lawrence
- Fearless leadership by Carey D. Lohrenz
- Start With Why by Simon Sinek
- The Energy Clock: 3 Simple Steps to Create a Life by Molly Fletcher

Understanding how successful organizations are built:
- 7 Attributes of Agile Growth by Keith Cupp and Andy Warren
- The Infinite Game by Simon Sinek
- Breakthrough Leadership by Mike Goldman
- Great by Choice by Jim Collins
- Turning the Flywheel by Jim Collins

www.ingramcontent.com/pod-product-compliance
Lightning Source LLC
LaVergne TN
LVHW010404070526
838199LV00065B/5892